What Lies Ahead

A Collection of Poems

Ed Krizek

What Lies Ahead
A Collection of Poems

© 2013, Ed Krizek

Cover photo: Emma Bordi
Cover design: Katherine Krizek
Book design: Jo-Anne Rosen

Second Printing, 2018
Manufactured in the United States of America

ISBN: 978-1-941066-34-8

Wordrunner Press
Petaluma, California

CONTENTS

Acknowledgements

"Fourth of July 2009," *This Light Will Fade* (Krizek), 2009

"Living Ghosts," *This Light Will Fade* (Krizek), 2009

"You Never Answered," *This Light Will Fade* (Krizek), 2009

"Perfect Ambition," *Hudson View*, 2010

"To a Life Unlived," *Cherry Blossom Review*, 2010

"Meditation on Buddhist Thought," *Buddhist Poetry Review*, 2011

"Shopping," *Mortal Thoughts* (Krizek), 2011

"Well-Dressed Man," *Mortal Thoughts* (Krizek), 2011

what lies ahead

SHARDS

I want
to put my shards of broken memory
together in a bowl,
run my hands through them
see what rises to the top.
Then do it again and again
until I can remember
the sound of the door slamming
in the padded room of the hospital.
The feeling of my body quivering
the first time I made love.

Mind shattered with a bad luck hammer
or perhaps a carelessly thrown stone
Sometimes the balm of nostalgia
soothes the wounds.
Sometimes they are as raw
and openly bleeding
as in the beginning.
Splinters of celebration
poke between gaps
in the debris.

Within the wreckage
I search for myself
never able to see
more than an eye, an arm, a torso.

What was I wearing
the day my father died?

I search for the tonic
of my past, not yet lost,
but slowly evaporating.
I guzzle the harsh liquid
stinking with used up opportunity
its taste reminiscent
of an overripe peach
fermenting on the tongue.

LIVING GHOSTS

For Kate

Sunlight reflects off the loopty-loop
as the roller coaster
filled with passengers
travels along gray rails.
You always liked the amusement piers.
I think I remember that.
I know you liked the shore.
The sounds and the smell
of the boardwalk
tickle my brain
with confusion.
I think I loved you
when we knew each other.
At that time I was never sure.

It's not simply the boardwalk
and the shore that brings you back.
Recollections fall out of life like
         dust
and cover over daily experiences
with a shroud of finality.
Images arise in my thoughts
triggered by some small twist.
They flow endlessly
like the bubbles rising
in a glass of beer.

It isn't that I miss you, exactly.
It's that I miss me.
I miss being young—
racing into a life of endless newness.

Perhaps it is this way for you.
Now instead of racing
into the future
we step slowly
as we contemplate the end.
We are living ghosts
in each other's thoughts.
Two specters that once had substance
but will float away
like a burnt offering
to the gods.

SHOPPING

I stay out of department stores.
Do not like shopping.
Do not like to be
seduced by rows of products
that call out like whores
manipulating me into wanting them.
Their packaging is so sexy!
Their placement so coy
yet inviting.
My lust for them
never ends.

I am going to shred
my charge card—
as soon as I pay it off.

I wonder
if there's a twelve-step program
for over-spenders.

I will check the internet
as soon as the new,
extra fast,
extra powerful computer
I ordered arrives.
It first appeared to me
on a highway billboard while speeding,
along with everyone else,
toward an unnamed destination
that I saw once on a TV show.

THE PRISONER

Encased in flesh and bone,
self-made, paralytic
he rolls up with a small book
resting on his arms.
Is this your work?
His response appears affirmative.

I read the poems:

People talk about Christmas
love, goodwill.
At the end of the day
most have gone home
to spouses and families.
He lies in bed alone
while a recording of
Silent Night
plays in the next room.

He writes from his urge
for self-expression,
creating art
typing one letter at a time.

Suicide bombers.
He wonders why people
with healthy, functioning bodies
would
blow themselves up?

I say
This is beautiful!
He seems pleased.

I try to speak to him
but find myself
talking to the man helping him,
the man who brought him here.
The man moves the prisoner
on to the next critic.
She has the temerity
to suggest changes.
Should I have been more attentive
to craft and word choice
rather than the transcendent humanness
of the work
which must touch
anyone who reads it?

My next day's mind
steeped in sales and marketing
remembers Mattie Stepanek,
the late boy poet
who died of a rare degenerative disease,
and whose books of poetry
were best sellers.
And Zsolt
who wrote eloquently
about life and love
as his body collapsed around him.

I decide to call the residence.
I speak excitedly to the man-helper
about possibilities,
offer my assistance.

But the man,
and all the prisoners
at the home

already know about
Mattie Stepanek,
and Zsolt,
and some others
I do not.

He tells me
the prisoner would rather
keep his dignity
than go on display.
He wants his work
to be judged on its merit,
to be understood
as a human being.
He won't sell himself
for money or fame like the rest of us
who walk about freely,
prisoners of our own greed
always for sale,
afraid to embrace
the truths of life
the way the prisoner
does daily,
one keystroke
at a time.

SUNDAY AFTERNOON

Flopping on the sofa
deflated
I try to focus on the now—
the comfort
of relationships
that ease my life.
Still I long
like a love struck
teenager
for something undefined.
Nostalgia
filters the present—
a residue
of disjointed episodes
appear desirable
to a collector of memories.
Vivid images
segments of time lost
the dead
all are displayed before me
John Coltrane
reaches out from the stereo.
The music is alive
a soundtrack
for my reverie.
Faces and events bubble
into my thoughts.
I do not know
how they are connected.
The music plays
and I drift
wondering who meant what to me.
As I lie restively

the reverie continues.
The present becomes the past
and time has no meaning.

YOU NEVER ANSWERED

For Sharon

You never answered
the letters I sent over the years.
I write them to a stranger,
a person you choose not to acknowledge,
one more misstep on the path.
During the good times you said,
I want to have your children.

That never happened.

Our life together ruptured
like an aneurysm
bleeding into both our guts.
We were a fertilized egg,
an embryo aborted by circumstance
and our increasing differences.
That fetus, no more
than a piece of decayed tissue now,
did exist once, before we surrendered
to maturity's current
and drowned ourselves
in good judgment and wisdom.

When a thing is dead
some simply bury the corpse
and let time and the worms have their way.
Others build monuments
or give large sums to charity.
Neither a builder, nor a philanthropist,
nonetheless
I honor a time which is inseparable from my psyche,

where there is a shadow cast by a marker
that stands among the many graves of my past.

Perhaps too there is a headstone
with my name on it in your memory
that you visit from time to time
and I have just never seen
the stones you leave behind.

FOURTH OF JULY 2009

1

Changed my hairstyle so many times,
I don't know what I look like.
                              —David Byrne

My home is outside Philly
where the empty brick factories
speak the poetry of lost hopes
while the city's tax base moves away
in search of the American dream.

Freedom—
I've come out of so many worlds
of searching.

Walking through suburban streets
I remember a riverside picnic
on a hot day
when the ants stayed away
and we stuffed ourselves with
the moment.
Afterward I read you a poem.
It was about choosing life.

I hear music when I walk.
It is the soundtrack of a chameleon's life.

I don't sound like anybody
said Elvis to the Colonel.

The King is dead
and buried in Graceland.

2

Everybody knows this is nowhere
               —Neil Young

In the locker room of The Boy's Club of Queens
I learned the rap of the streetwise.
Who?
You momma.
Let's not get on mothers,
'cause I been on yours for a week!
Competition—
Word tricks
designed to create
a pecking order
among the toughs.
We all believed
there was someplace better to be.

Driving through
burnt out neighborhoods
with my doors locked
I see the homeboys
sitting on stoops,
or smoking on the street corner
with quart bottles
wrapped in brown paper bags
and miss
the love that comes
from acceptance.

3

Fountain of sorrow, fountain of life,
you've known that hollow sound
of your own steps in flight
                                    —*Jackson Browne*

When I was young
I did not believe in impermanence.
I could swim the 400
faster than any high schooler
in New York City or Jersey.

My father died.

I wore his winter overcoat
and a brown Kangol cap
speckled with yellow paint
to swim meets in the cold weather.

I have an old black & white picture of him
in a cabinet full of bric-a-brac.
He looks at the world sadly.
When I see his expression
I understand his pain.

I surround him
with medals, diplomas, plaques,
I have earned.
He continues to stare
at something unseen
in the distance.

4

During Business School
I owned one navy, and one gray
pin-striped suit.
Red ties.
White shirts.
Worked in Midtown
for an investment bank
and thought a lot
about money.

At my grandfather's funeral
I asked my father's brother
how he and my father
had made money
in the construction business.

He said simply,
We stole it.

5

I'm just sittin' here
watchin' the wheels
go 'round and 'round
          —John Lennon

In a low rent motel
near Lake Winnepesaukee
I play jazz
on my ghetto blaster.
Snippets and images
from the path
that led me here
rise and fall
like swells
in some great ocean.
The sun is shining
in a cloudless blue sky.
Yesterday I bought
a rubber raft.
Today I will inflate it,
take it down to the lake,
and float
where the wind
and waves take me.

6

Be here now!
          —Baba Ram Dass

In the White Mountains
the taste of the air,
sweet in my mouth,
reminds me of weekends
on Little Peconic Bay
when I was a boy.

I am staying in a luxury hotel
where the guests are pampered.
Two person Jacuzzi—
chocolate chip cookies on my pillow at night.
My wife is shopping for antiques
while I sit with a double espresso.

Still, I have the urge to smoke cigarettes,
listen to street corner singers,
and drink warm beer from a quart bottle
wrapped in a brown paper bag.

I contemplate dinner—
18 year old single malt,
oysters on the half shell,
free range duck
enhanced with a glass of wine.

I read
poetry, literary fiction, Buddhist philosophy—

Life
is the mystical experience.

FROM MEMORY

Your face, now ash
forms like a specter in my thoughts.
The blue place
on your right leg haunts me too.
Your hair, your teeth, your eyes,
dusted into earth
appear like wisps in the pit of night.
Sinking, my fear rises up.
There will be no more quiet talks,
no more laughter, or small words of encouragement.
Like Houdini I want to bring you back.
for one more conversation.
Your favorite pictures
still cover the white walls.
Your books are in their shelves.
Your bed is made.
The sheet music
you used to play from
has been donated to schools..
When you visit in my wishful dreams,
we will have to play the music from memory.

HAPPINESS IN A CAN

Waiting for the sun's globe
to drop into the Gulf
I think I am the luckiest man
in the world
vacationing at the beach in Florida
amidst the herons, egrets,
dolphins, and manatees.
I snap photos
trying to record this feeling
preserve it for times
of sadness, despair
as if it were possible
to capture happiness
store it and draw down
on the inventory
when I need a pick-me-up
the way television commercials
tell us to drink cans of beer.

People say
there are sharks in these waters
but I have never seen them.
They frequent the deep shadows.
But I am not concerned.
Like most of America
I swim in the shallows.

Some of our best minds
are trying to find ways
to put happiness in a can.
They want to sell it
become richer than they already are.
Everyone wants to drink something,

eat something, or take a pill
to be happy.

I keep snapping photos until dark
and consider staying out
to see the moon and stars.
But as night begins
dark streamlined shapes move in
from where they have been
patiently waiting.

I shiver
although the breeze is warm, friendly.
I decide to return
to my hotel room
where I can view my photos
in someplace that appears safe.

A WREATH FOR EDDIE

I was named, "Edwin"
after my father.
My mother called him, "Eddie".
He was young
when he died at forty-four.
For thirty-five years
until her death
my mother paid
a local florist
to place a wreath
on his grave at Christmas.

Neither she nor I
visited the grave much.
When we did
we could see
these decaying remnants
of remembrance.

I hadn't been to
my father's grave for years
when my mother passed.
When I found the florist's bill
I called the number
told them to stop.

Now it is Christmas again.
I seek out relatives
and old friends
trying to find our connection.
Still I feel something's awry.

My mother is not in the plot with my father.
She wanted her ashes scattered
in Glacier National Park.
He is two thousand miles away
in New York City.
But can see his marble monument
as I smoke cigarettes
at night on my balcony
in twenty degree Pennsylvania weather.
I look up at the stars
and consider our planet's smallness
my own existence.
I want to touch something
I'm not sure is there.
I think of the unspoiled snow
in Glacier that comforts my Mom.
I remember Eddie,
the man she loved.
In the morning I call the cemetery
and have a wreath placed
at the foot of his
rose-colored stone.

MENDING THE QUILT

We are scarred
and alive
hoping for a clue
as to who we are.
We measure and cut
patch and sew.
Longing
binds together
pieces rent
by circumstance
and strain.

To find material
we look up old friends
who don't remember us
or worse
whose memories clash
with ours.
Our shared experiences
are stitched together
bound by the psychic glue
of need.
We must repair to understand.

We assemble lives
from a blueprint
found somewhere
in a dream.
We leave a collage
behind for those
who loved us.
They use it
to stay the coldness
of our departure.

BAKER'S LAMENT

Remembering the past
is like baking a cake
with no recipe.
I sift through ingredients
that present themselves
like cold molasses:
sweet, sticky, viscous, or slippery
trying to find the right combination
that will create some sort
of marvel.
There are no
predefined guidelines.
A chef considers components
but often, after a long night
of trial and error
the end result
is undefined
a congealed morass
with substance but no form
involving too much guesswork
to prepare anything
remotely appealing
to a hungry heart.

ALMOST ACQUAINTED

I don't know how
the unshaven man
holding a sign that says
Homeless
came to be standing
on the corner
where a traffic light
controls the flow of commuters
leaving the city.
I look away
from his blue eyes.
retreating into my car
as if painted steel and auto glass
could protect me
from becoming like him.

He must have started life
like all of us
a helpless child
dependent on the good
will of others
for survival.
Once again dependent
he implores the more fortunate
for spare change
invoking guilt
then fear.

He may have once had a family
a wife perhaps a child
maybe a job.
But I don't really know.
I wave my hand

and stare at the road ahead
when he taps my window.
He moves
down the line of stopped cars.

It seems like an hour
before the light changes.
I quickly move my foot
from brake to gas
and drive a little too fast
to the suburbs.

TO A LIFE UNLIVED

In Memory of Paul Edward Allard
11/25/50 – 4/19/69

In the spring of 1969
I was in ninth grade
advanced for my age.
Paul Edward Allard was fighting in Vietnam.
I didn't know him,
nor did I know any of the soldiers
whose graves I view
as I stand in this cemetery
today, Memorial Day 2010.

In my hand I hold
a bouquet of red roses
and lilies.
Lilies for the dead.
Fields of waving flags
mark the lives of so many.
As I look across the meadow.
I wonder if anyone knows
how many are here.
The fight is over for them.
It ended before they planned.
What is left of their hopes
lies here.

But let us, the survivors not
be overcome.
Whether or not they died nobly
or just as an artifact of violence
they died for something
greater than themselves.

Perhaps they were heroes
righteously storming enemy guns.
Perhaps they just wanted
to do their duty to God and country.

Maybe they were just
poor frightened bastards
unable or unwilling to flee to Canada.

I was never in Vietnam,
never served in the military.
I was in the last year of the lottery.
My number was over 300.
My girlfriend checked.
I was young and felt immortal.
If my number had been called
I would have served.

When you are young
you stand by your ideals.
You stand up for what you believe,
right or wrong,
Through our struggle we learn
that God, if He exists,
may have His own agenda
and not be on our side at all.
You live through pain and fear
not of death, but of life.
Yet you know you are lucky
not to be lying in a green field
with a flag waving over your head.

As the honor guard offers its salute
to the fallen and the bugler blows taps,
I look down on the flowers

on Paul Edward Allard's grave.
He died April 19, 1969.
My tearful gaze falls
on a group of unopened lilies
in the bouquet and I weep
for his life,
a life that was never lived.

WELL-DRESSED MAN

I have to go to a funeral today.
Hope my suit fits.
There's nothing
like a well-fitted suit
to make you feel
like you're a comfort to the family.
Of course the corpse
will be dressed in a suit.
Some think
an open casket is barbaric,
but I feel a connection
to both the living
and the dead on these occasions.
A connection to the living
because
there is nothing like
sitting in a room with a corpse
to make you feel alive.
A connection to the dead
because
they look their best
better than they have ever looked.

When I face the angel of death
I'm sure he will be wearing a well-cut suit
(probably custom made).
He will tap me on the shoulder
Come along, you, he will say.
Since I am now closer
to that time
I buy a new suit
every year
to make sure I'm ready

for my final day.
As I lie in my coffin
I will look good,
feel nothing.

HOMECOMING

1

I returned to Eden
        to find a race of homogeneous
 androgynous cannibals
        waiting dinner for me at McDonald's.
I was coming home to no home
        from a long trip to nowhere special
        because who am I? What can I see
        that you can't? My eyes are no different
        from yours — all rods and cones and retina
        and vitreous humor and aqueous humor.
So when I tell you I saw Hell,
        you can see it too unless you are blind
        and of course if you are blind
        you will be fair when you judge my story
        For justice is blind and so it follows
        that the blind are just.
Li Young I too am a refugee.
        My childhood home is gone
        with the evaporation of time and place.

2

My bisexual friend tells me
        that whether he watches
        a homo or hetero skin flick
        on Saturday night depends on his mood—
        maybe it's just like how the weather is
        or the time of year. He told me
        that if I still looked like my college picture
        he would want to fuck me.

It's been many years since college
It's been many years too since I lived in California.
I wasn't very happy there,
but I got laid a lot.
Then I went crazy—
raving, unspeakably crazy.
wound up in a padded room
in the psycho ward.
I told them in the hospital
that the CIA and the FBI were doing things to me.
Then I asked for a tomato sandwich.
I thought my ex lover was attending orgies
and not inviting me.
Actually, I've never been to an orgy.
Have you?
Don't answer that.
Ain't nobody's business
if you do.

3

Released from the mental hospital
traveled east to the New York City suburbs.
I tried to be myself.
I was no one. Lived with my mother
who thought there was nothing
wrong with me.
Believed my life was over. Took
my father's old shotgun to the ammo store.
They sold me shells that fit.
Not wanting to dirty the house
went out to my mother's backyard
loaded the gun and put the barrel
in my mouth.

One awful instant of pain—
  Didn't pull the trigger out of concern for her.
  Later in a fit of rage and agony smashed the shotgun
  on a brick wall in her house.

4

Moved to Philadelphia to make a home for myself.
  Ran out of money
   moved to an attic apartment
  on the third floor of a twin.
My landlord was a British woman who later
  married a Black Muslim.
  She began wearing a burka
  Her husband laid his prayer
  rug on the living room floor.
  I walked past him as he prayed
  on my way to my flat in the late afternoons.
Enchanted stayed there seven years
  walking up three flights of stairs
  several times a day
  listening to the pipes groan
  thinking they were talking to me
  every month afraid I wouldn't make the rent.

5

When I left my mother's house
  for the first time I threw off her love
  and followed the direction of the wind.
I saw friends with
  the love of their families and secretly envied them.
I drifted to the rooms filled
  with pot smoke and Quaalude induced stupors
  and meaningless sex and my heart was broken.

I tried to find permanence in vapid friendships
          and in the families of others
          only to be ostracized.

6

More than two decades have passed—

I have returned from the trip which started as tangential thought
          one night after several rounds of scotch
          the trip that blossomed into a morass
          of Daliesque images and Rimbaud-like dreams

I have returned from the isolation of loveless delusion.

I have come home to you my darling for without you
          there is no love and no life.
I have come home to say that
          the mind baffling paranoid psychotic trip—
The trip where I lost reality and found my path to you
          was worth it.

PERFECT AMBITION

For Caroline

Sunny rain drips wet light
through the trees
a rainbow
in the morning air.

A Cardinal sings for life.
Two gray squirrels sprint
up an oak tree, around the grass
their small lungs gasping

I throw open a window
resin from thousands of dead cigarettes
my lungs fill with life.

Thoughts of great deeds
disperse like an oppressive haze
in an offshore wind
as you lie sleeping
in the bed
where we made love
last night.

Quietly I brew
a pot of coffee.
A new scent
fills the room
and charms me,
calms me.

I fill your cup
and place it next to mine
on the wooden table..

I wake you.
We drink our coffee
together
as the day begins.

MY FATHER'S WAKE

His open casket rested
at the front of a large low lit room
filled with folding chairs.
Dark stained wood surrounded
cushions of white satin
that held him.
Sunken and still
his body lay
as though he were napping face up
wearing his best suit.
Calloused hands scrubbed clean
protruded from the ends of the sleeves
of his white shirt.
Underneath the make up
I thought I could see the bruise
on his face where he landed
after the twenty foot fall
that broke his neck.
I recall that the pastor
who eulogized him said he died
while doing the work he loved—
building something.
I found that thought pleasing
but was not ready to hear
my school friends' and family's condolences
followed by vacuous discussions of the weather.
It seemed as though they were speaking
in an alternate universe
one where the people I loved died painlessly
of old age and things always worked out.

ONE CHILD

At five years old
you don't want
your friends
to see you
kissing your mother
good-bye
when she takes you to school.
Public displays are unseemly
and embarrassing at that age.
You look to make sure
no one can see
before you apply a peck
to her cheek.

Good-bye Mommy.

At five you want to hide
the links to the woman
who gave you life
who always managed
to make you feel better
even when the school bully
pushed you into a mud puddle
one Sunday after church
or when as an adult
you doubted you would regain
your sanity after years
of mistrust and ineffective medications.

At *fifty*-five
with her ashes scattered
your feel her presence
when you handle

the music box
shaped like a miniature piano
or when your eye happens
upon a photograph
of her smiling
that you casually placed
on top of the television.
She rises
in your thoughts like hot steam
as you drink tea
from her favorite French mug.
You kiss its rim
not sure
if the heat will burn
or if you will feel
her cheek on your lips.

MEDITATION ON BUDDHIST THOUGHT

In the room I forgot
...the closet sags
with the sudden weights
of regret
        From "Thistles" by Philip Levine

When I was young
I promised myself
I would never forget
what being young
felt like.
The first time
I fell in love
I expected to love forever.
When I was mad
I thought
I would never be sane again.
Now I find time
has worn away parts of me
the way wind and water
erode the permanence of stone.
Tokens of remembrance
hang on my walls
like museum artifacts.
They speak in metaphor
of struggle, love, pain.
I see these trophies,
remember
where they came from
but cannot feel
their potency
nor the exaltation
and angst spent

in their acquisition.
Time has passed—
I am older
have lived longer.
Perhaps this is the way
of the end—
slowly
losing a piece
or two.

WHAT LIES AHEAD

Looking back in the distance
from a place of relative safety
the way through the woods
seems like a labyrinth
of twists and turns
with animals ready to kill
or maim
hiding in darkness.

I wonder what golden thread
led me here.

Hard traveling over years
often caused me to mistake
the appearance of a rest stop
for a final destination.

Now no longer youthful
I cling
to past joys
as if to a life ring
in an ocean of shadows.

Looking ahead
I'm not sure
if I see a two-tailed demon
or just a youngster
flying a kite
in a summer breeze.
It floats in the air like a dancer.

ED KRIZEK BIO

Ed Krizek was born in New York City and now runs a sales and marketing business in Swarthmore, PA, a suburb of Philadelphia. He holds a BA and MS from University of Pennsylvania, and an MBA and MPH from Columbia University. He is a member of the Unitarian Universalist Church of Delaware County, has published over fifty-five articles, poems and short stories in various publications, and won prizes in several poetry and short story competitions. You can see more of his work at www.edkrizekwriting.com.

www.ingramcontent.com/pod-product-compliance
Lightning Source LLC
Chambersburg PA
CBHW022343040426
42449CB00006B/699